Doodle Art

Inspiring Your Creativity

Written and Illustrated by

Harriet Hodgson

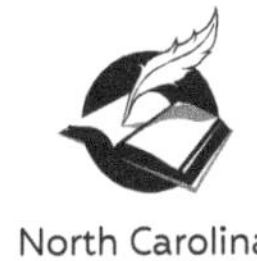

North Carolina

Published in the United States by WriteLife Publishing
(an imprint of Boutique of Quality Books Publishing Company, Inc.)
www.writelife.com

978-1-60808-307-7 (p)
978-1-60808-308-4 (e)

Cover and book design by Robin Krauss, www.bookformatters.com

Contents

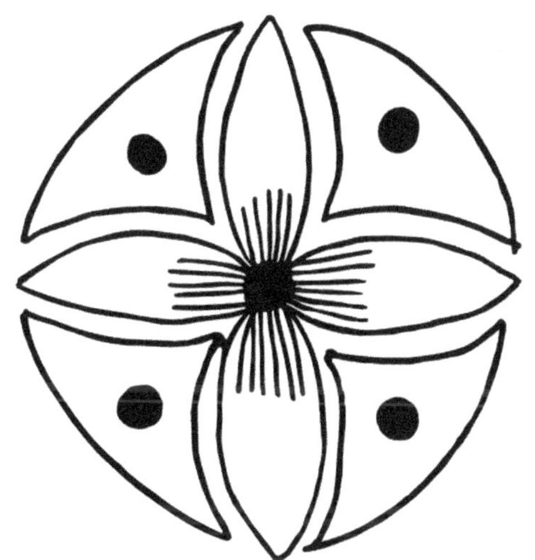

Part 1

Everybody Doodles

After researching doodling for years, I decided it's instinctive. The urge to doodle seems to be part of our makeup. Whether we do neat doodles or crooked ones, we doodle when we're waiting, bored, or antsy. Everybody doodles, even you.

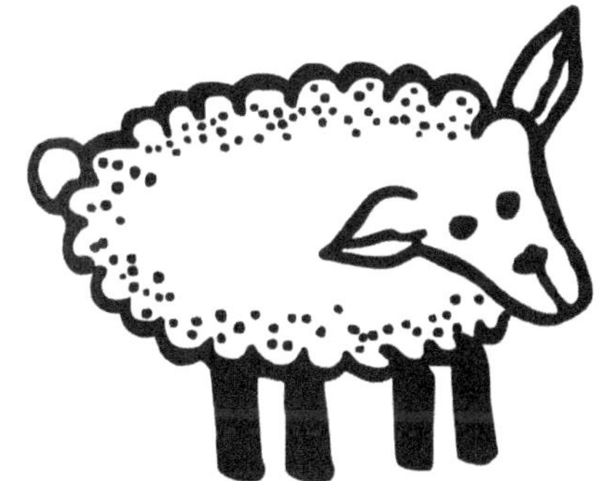

Doodling is a hot topic these days. You see it in advertising, on all sorts of commercial products (textiles, dishware, clothing, wall art) and more. One of the best things about doodling is that you can do it anywhere and at any time. Better yet, doodling is appropriate for all ages, from great grandparents like me, to toddlers, to school kids.

When Joe Whale, an eight-year boy from Shrewsbury, England, kept doodling at school, his teacher complained to his parents. Rather than being annoyed or punishing Joe, his parents signed him up for art classes. Joe's art teacher was impressed with his talent and told others about it.

A local restaurant heard about Joe and asked him to decorate its plain white interior. As Joe doodled up and down walls and around corners, the restaurant was transformed. Joe is older now and his work hangs in art galleries. He has designed sneakers for Nike, written and illustrated books about doodling, and has a website worth visiting, https://thedoodleboy.com

While this is an amazing story, you have your own story to tell, and doodling helps you tell it. Doodling is relaxing and gives you breaks from whatever is going on in your life. Feeling eager? Doodle. Feeling bored? Doodle. Feeling sad? Doodle.

Fun is the main reason to doodle. Some are doodling on old newspapers, sheet music, and gift wrapping paper. Others are merging their work with watercolors and collage materials. The doodling possibilities are almost endless, and many options are open to you.

Keep on doodling. The techniques and patterns within these pages can help you create countless doodles. Every doodle is an expression of you.

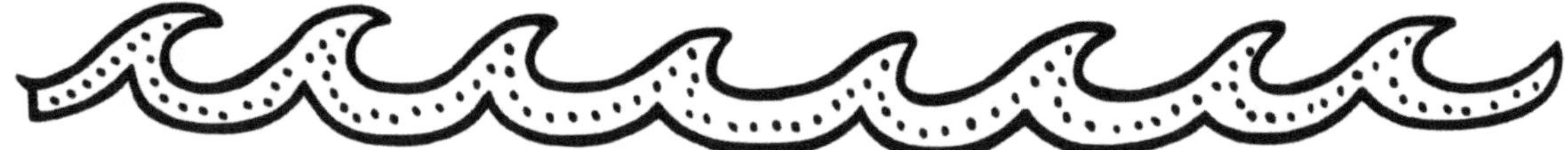

Part 2

Gather These Things

1. **Something to doodle with:** colored pencils, crayons, or Flair felt tip pens of various colors. Stay away from permanent markers because they contain toxic solvents which can harm your health if inhaled long-term without proper ventilation. Permanent markers can also be harmful when absorbed through the skin.

2. **A cookie cutter.** The shape of the cookie cutter should be instantly recognizable, such as a star, heart, flower or butterfly.

3. **Your natural creativity.** "But I'm not artistic," you may mumble to yourself. "I can't draw a straight line." Thankfully, you don't need straight lines to doodle. Crooked, wonky lines make your doodles unique. Don't worry about staying inside the lines because you're doodling.

You may be wondering about doodling paper. I like to use Strathmore Artist Tiles, a 6-inch by 6-inch square pad of paper with perforated pages that can be torn out. This pad fits into my purse and the pages are just the right size for doodling while waiting.

Gather your supplies, find a comfortable chair, take a deep breath and begin. You're doodling for you—and nobody else—so let your imagination soar!

— Part 3 —

What's a Doodle?

The Merriam-Webster online dictionary defines doodle as "an aimless scribble, design, or sketch." Wikipedia defines the word as a "drawing while a person's attention is otherwise occupied." New definitions define doodle as an easy, safe way to express emotions.

Because the heart shape appears often in doodles, I define doodle as a combination of ordinary doodling, comic techniques, and folk art. This definition includes scribble art.

Scribbles are one of the first shapes young children make. Once they're used to scribbling, kids name their scribbles and tell stories about them. While the stories may not be understandable, you get a sense of meaning via facial expressions, gestures and voice.

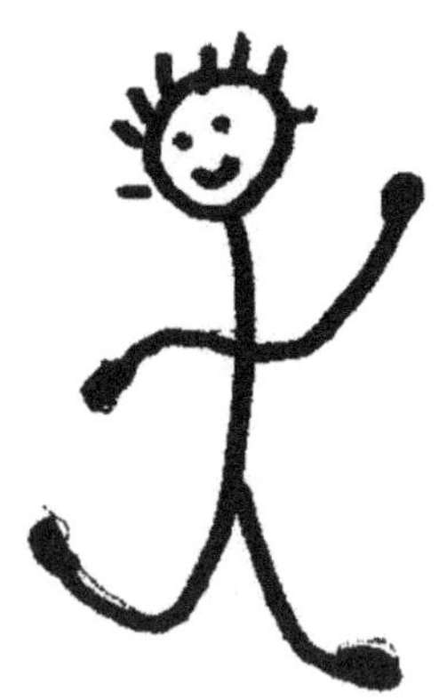

Doodle a scribble on the next page. Your scribble may be wound like a ball of yarn or expanded with curves, angles, and zig-zags. It's your call.

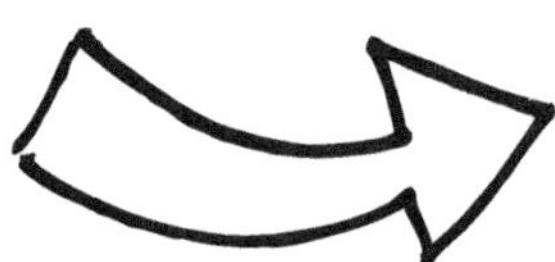

Part 4

Doodling Isn't New

Humans have been doodling for centuries. Some experts consider ancient cave paintings as doodles, but other experts disagree. So far, the cave paintings that have been discovered are mostly animals, and they're more drawings than doodles.

Ancient people in Australia drew doodles in sand. According to a BBC article by David Robinson, "Are We Hard-Wired to Doodle?" most of the sand doodlers were women. Their doodles were a language and included symbols. A U shape, for example, symbolized a person sitting cross-legged. A small u inside a large U symbolized a child sitting on a mother's lap.

Language was combined with doodling, a subject that continues to intrigue researchers. One researcher found a 73,000-year-old doodle in a South African cave. The doodle was made with an ochre crayon, a mineral mixed with clay. The doodler drew something we draw today—a tic-tac-toe shape. Wow!

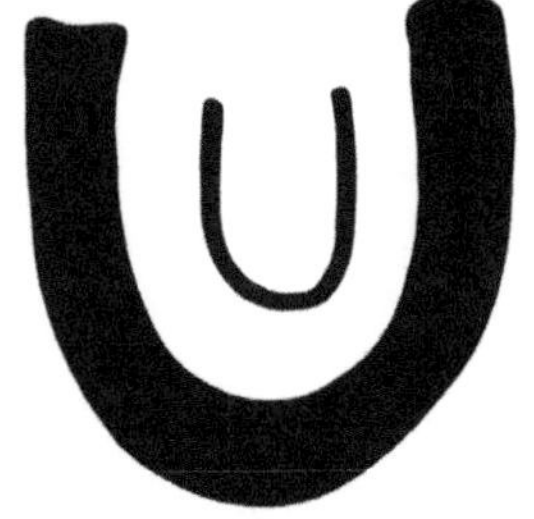

Doodle tic-tac-toe lines on the next page. Make some with straight lines and some with slanted lines like hashtags.

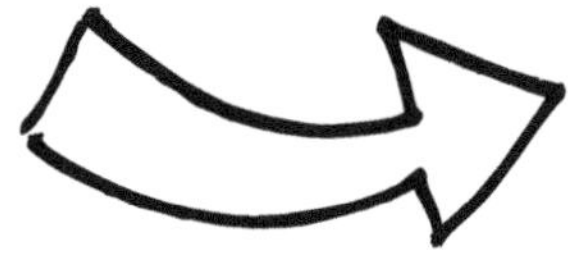

Part 5

Six Types of Doodling

1. **Stendoodling** (Starting with stencils and finishing with doodles). Since you may not have stencils on hand, I suggest using cookie cutters instead.

2. **Zen Doodling** (A calming approach with repeat patterns). Repeat is the key word here because repeating is relaxing, and we all need quiet, relaxed times in a day.

3. **Zentangles**© (Abstract form of doodling with structured patterns and no erasing). Rick Roberts and Maria Thomas came up with the idea and copyrighted it. They give workshops on Zentangles and certify attendees as teachers.

4. **Mandalas** (A planned doodle, most often circles with repetitive designs, but can be any shape; created to promote mindfulness). The mandala is a world-wide symbol.

5. **Scribble Art** (This is as free as it gets.) Artist Saul Steinberg (1914–1999), famous for his "New Yorker Magazine" drawings, made a scribble art doodle and put a face and hand holding the scribbling pen in the middle. See this amazing drawing on the Saul Steinberg Foundation website, https://saulsteinbergfoundation.org/search-artwork/page/3/

6. **Doodle Art (combines all the types listed above)** This book is about doodle art in general, how you can do it, and why to keep doing it. You're starting out on a doodle adventure.

Part 6

Benefits of Doodling

- While you're doodling, your mind is still working—gathering facts, solving problems, and more. You may not know your mind is processing, but it is.

- Doodling can make you pay close attention, or what's called Mindful Doodling. For example, while you're doodling a flower, you may focus on the shape of the petals.

- Surprisingly, doodling can improve memory.
  One study showed those who doodled in class remembered more than those who didn't doodle. This may have been because doodling kept tired or bored students awake.

- Sitting quietly and doodling helps you release feelings like anxiety, anger, and grief.

- Doodling is creative. Though this type of art may seem mindless, the opposite is true, and your mind is working in different ways.

- Doodling can help you know yourself. New ideas may come to mind while you're doodling.

- When you doodle, you get a peek at your subconscious mind in action. Indeed, your doodles may surprise you and that's amazing.

- Doodling can be a spiritual experience. Some meditate while they're doodling, and others pray. You may do both.

- Best of all, doodling is fun because there are no mistakes. If a line veers you just make it part of your doodle. Now that's something to celebrate! Doodle a smiley face here.

Part 7

Highlighting One Technique

Famous artists and doodle artists often focus on one technique to add interest and power to their work. This was true of Vincent Van Gogh, the artist who painted Starry Night. His oil painting, replete with swirling clouds of blue, grabs your attention. Whether you realize it or not, your eyes keep going back to the swirling clouds again and again.

Starry Night has a fascinating history. According to the Van Gogh Gallery website, Van Gogh painted the picture while he was living at the asylum of Saint-Paul-de-Mausole. He was sent there after cutting off his ear. Though Van Gogh was free to roam the facility, he didn't paint in his room. Starry Night is the view from Van Gogh's room, and he painted the scene from memory. To complete the picture, he added an imaginary village beneath the swirling clouds.

Van Gogh had hallucinations and suffered from epileptic fits. This may explain how and why he painted the clouds. Whatever the reason, Starry Night is one of the world's most famous paintings. If you visit the Van Gogh website, https://www.vangoghgallery.com.painting.starry-night, you may download a Starry Night picture to color. The swirling clouds are clearly outlined.

Joe Whale, the doodle artist described earlier, also highlights various techniques in his work. In his book, *The Official Doodle Boy Coloring Book*, one picture shows tiny, repetitive round people, tiny raindrops with eyes, and lightening shapes at the bottom. The blurb for the book tells us a little about the artist.

"When I doodle it makes me feel like the most happy person in the world," Joe admits, "because I can express myself fully as there is no right or wrong in art." Just as Joe says, there is no right or wrong doodle art that highlights a technique. You are in creative company, Vincent Van Gogh and Joe Whale, to name a few.

The following pages show examples of highlighting a single technique in doodle art: stippling, spirals, loops, repetitive lines, broken lines, double outlining, dot outlining and scribbles. There are blank pages for you to create your own doodle art with highlights. Think of the technique you may highlight and turn this imaginary picture into reality. You are a doodle artist!

Techniques and Patterns

Frequent doodlers rely on their favorite patterns. Of course, each doodler adds their own ideas and flourishes to a drawing. The following pages focus on shapes and patterns and practicing them—techniques that may jump-start your creativity.

Circle

The circle is the most common shape in doodling. Fill this big circle with small circles. Add color to each circle.

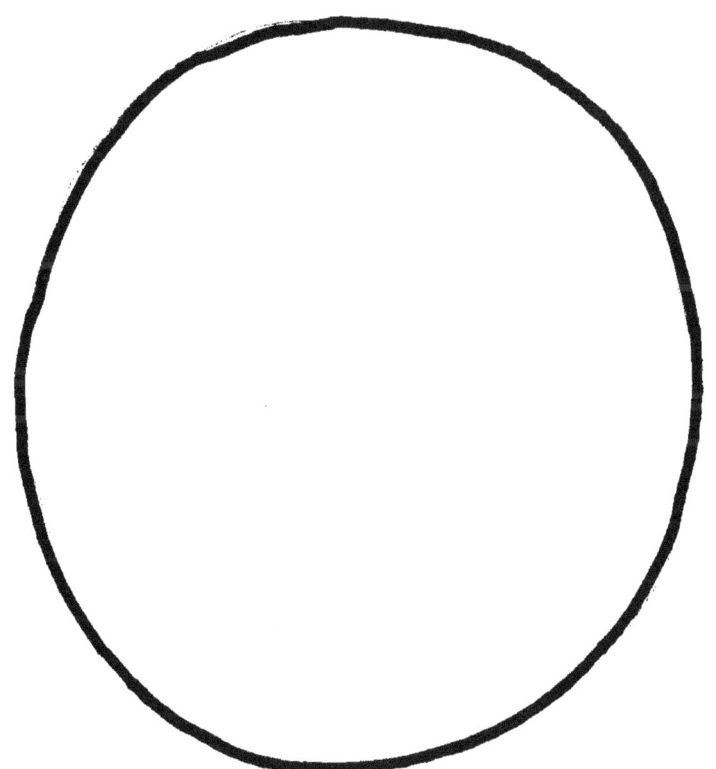

Bunches of Circles

Draw circles around this shape. Fill the page with circles—big ones, small ones, and wobbly ones. Brighten the circles with different colors.

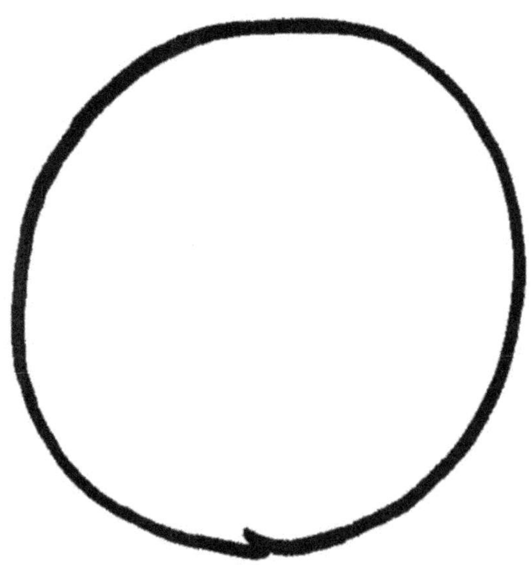

Spirals

Spirals are centuries old. This circle has a spiral in the middle. Doodle more circles with spirals.

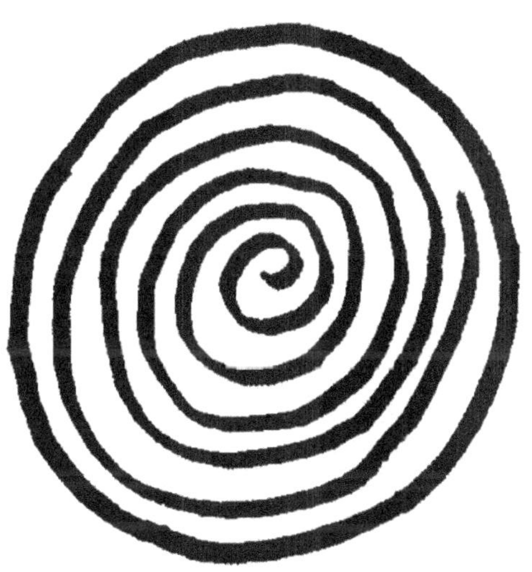

Spiral Flowers

Add a stem, dots, leaves, spirals to these circles to make flowers. Draw more flowers and create a garden.

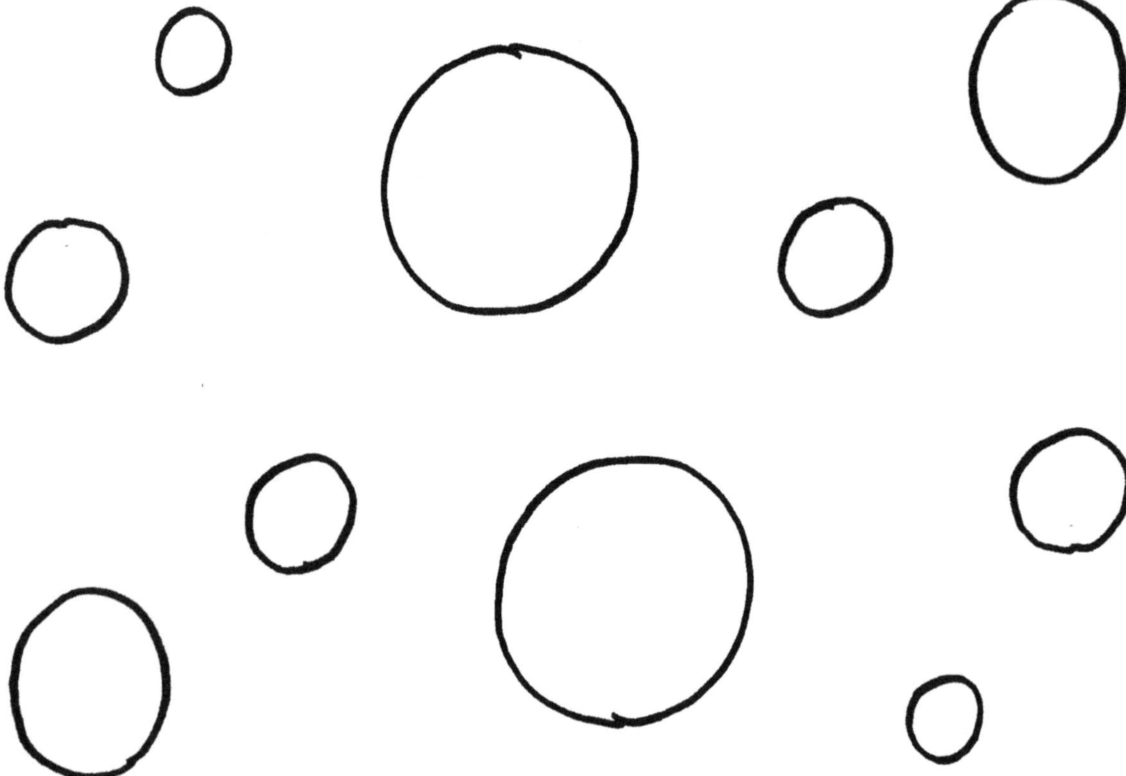

Stendoodle

Stendoodles begin with stencils, but you're going to use a cookie cutter. Hold the cutter firmly and trace around the rim. Decorate the cookie with dots, circles, and spirals.

Geometric Shapes

Add colors to these geometric shapes. Use the brightest colors you have. Now doodle your own geometric shape design.

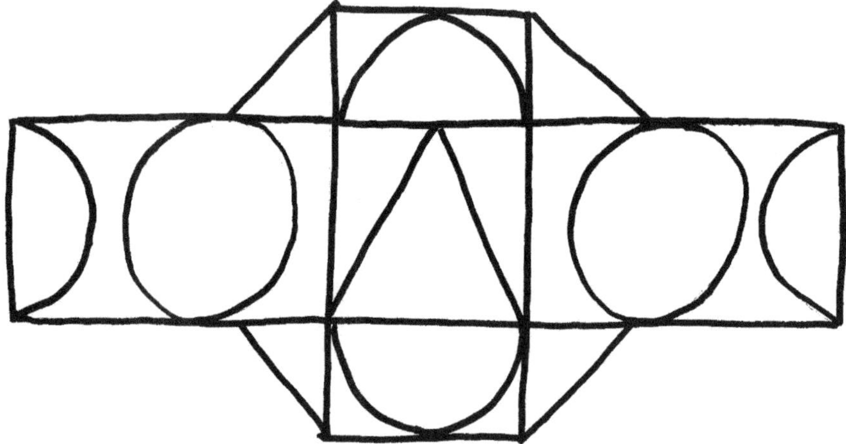

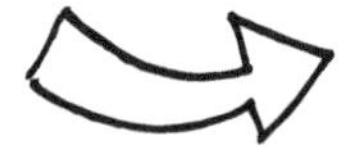

Repetitive Lines

Make lines beneath these lines. Go slowly and let your mind wander. Keep drawing lines. If a line is wobbly, draw the same wobbly line beneath the one above. Fill the page with lines. You're a Zen doodler!

Broken Lines

B roken lines are fun to doodle. Doodle broken lines raining down on this umbrella. Now add color and patterns. You're a Zen doodler again.

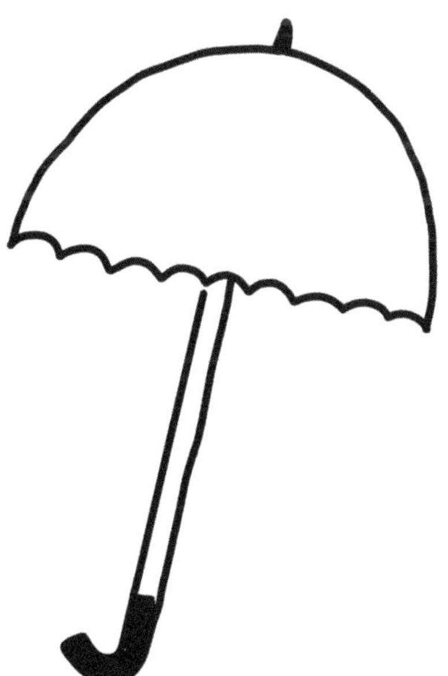

Mindful Doodling

Finish these triangles by starting at a point and drawing more lines as shown. Mindful doodling can help you focus on one thought and, at the same time, provide chances for your mind to wander.

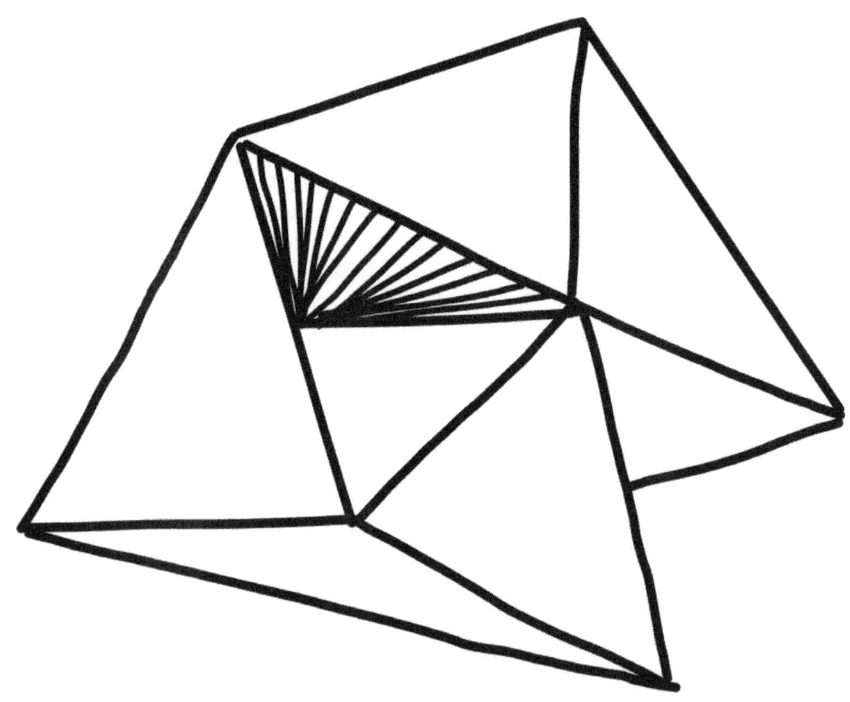

Stippling

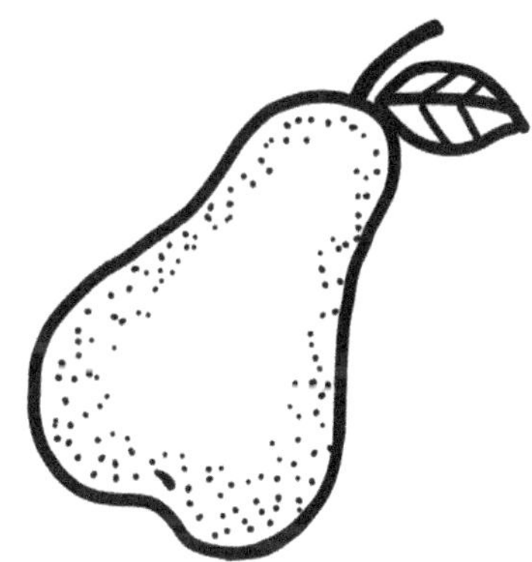

T iny dots—a technique called stippling—are used to shape images. This pear is an example of stippling. Draw more fruit and add stippling dots.

Loops

Loops seem to be instinctive and are part of doodling. Add more loops to the frame and doodle a picture inside.

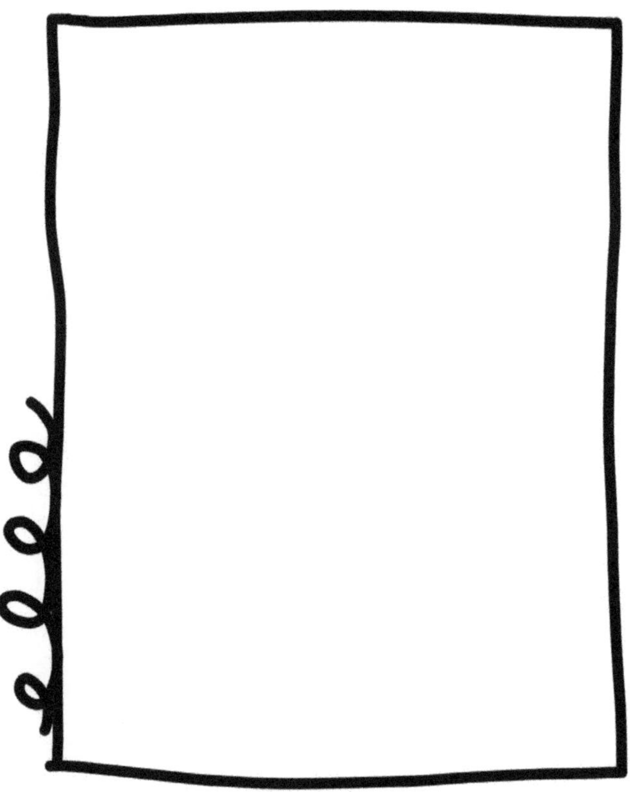

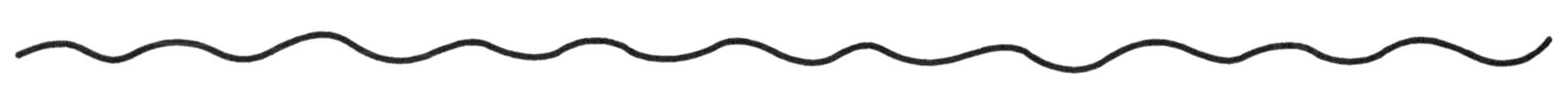

Connecting Shapes

Connect these squares with loops, lines, or dotted lines. When you've finished, brighten the squares with different colors.

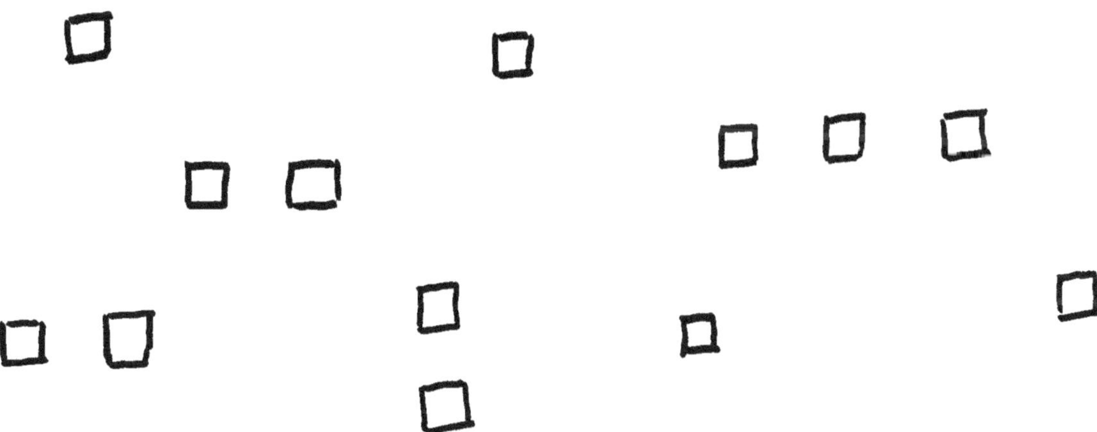

Hatching

Hatching—small lines going in the same direction—is another way to shape images. Doodle hatching lines on the second cloud and a rainbow between them. Decorate the rainbow with circles, spirals, lines, dots, and flowers.

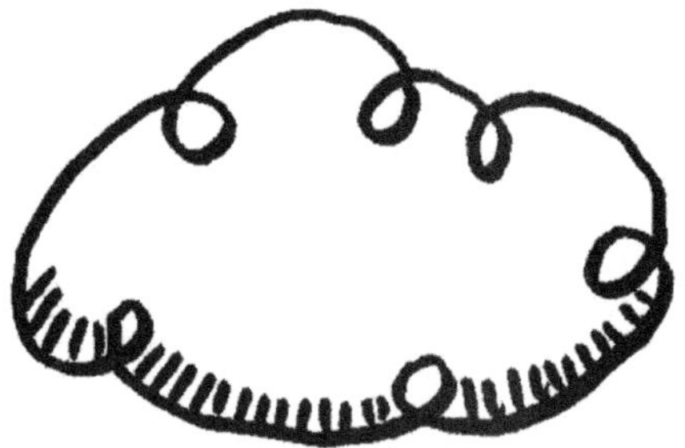 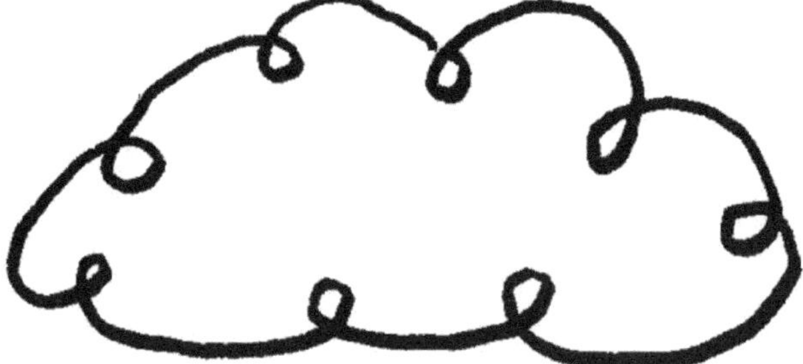

Cross Hatching

Cross hatching is a technique with lines going in opposite directions. Some doodle artists like to color the squares like a checkboard. Add color to the vase and doodle some flowers in it.

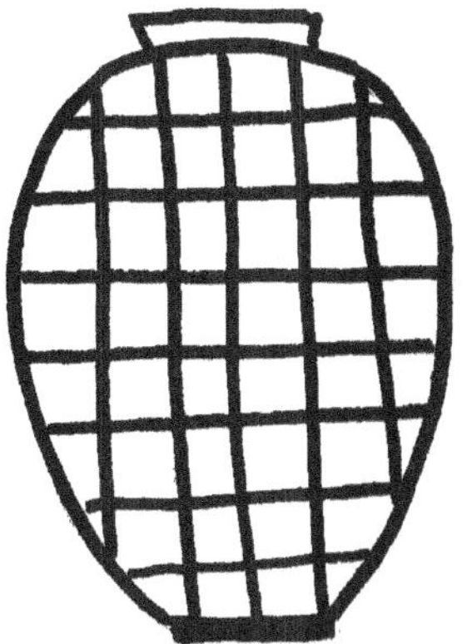

Weaving

This technique involves repetitive lines going in opposite directions. Continue the weaving pattern down the page.

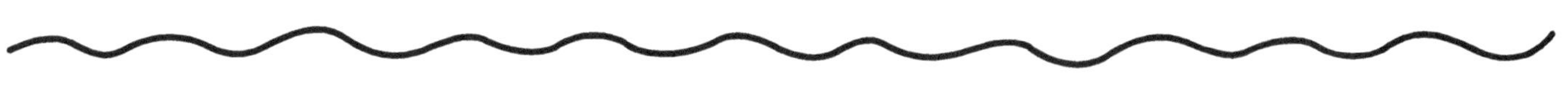

Curls

Curls—wavy lines that go up and down—make doodles interesting. Fill this square with curls of different colors.

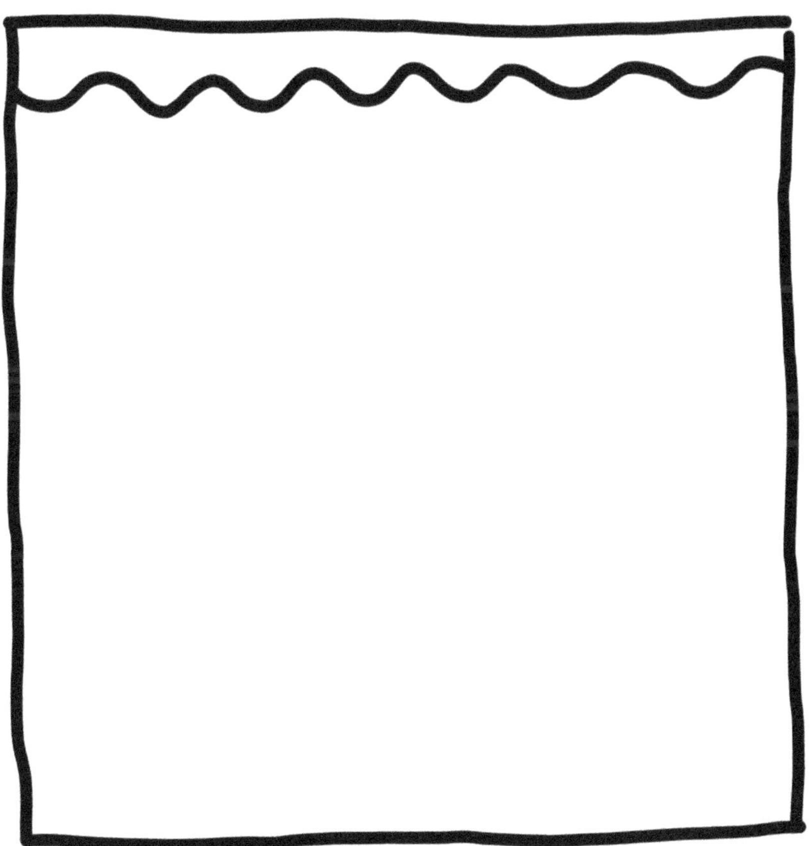

Continuous Line

You can get so good at doodling your pencil, pen, crayon, or marker never leaves the paper. This is called Continuous Line Doodling. Finish this picture with a continuous line.

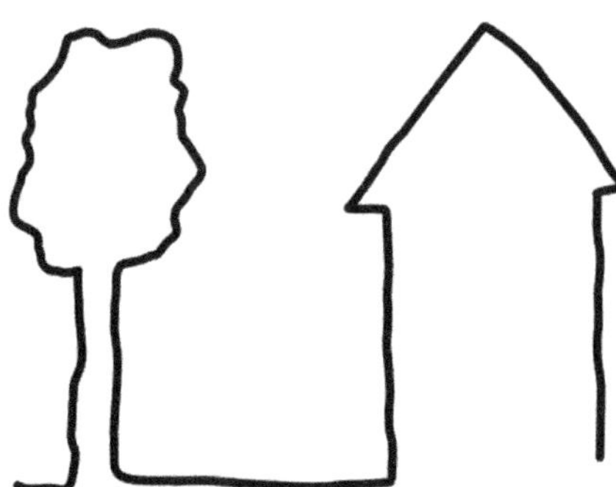

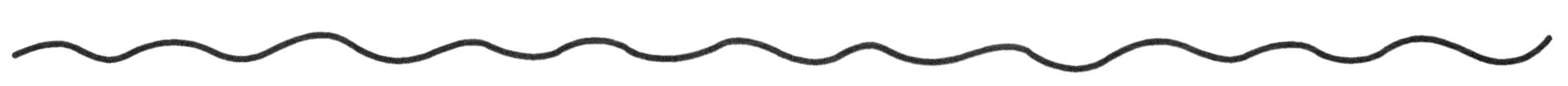

Lines Make Patterns

Lines can be anything and go anywhere. Fill these squares with lines that make patterns. Make each square different.

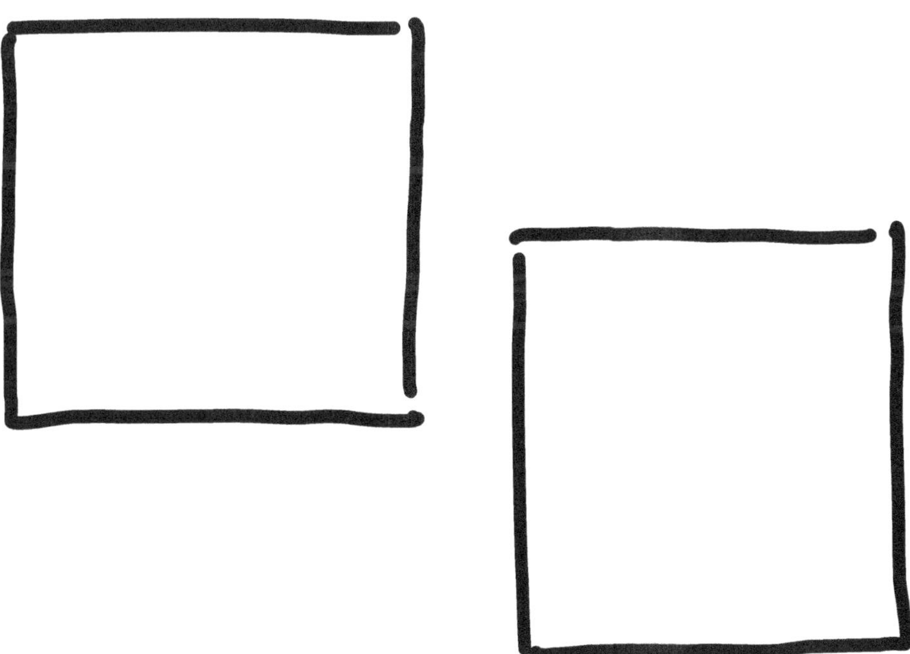

Finish the Doodle

It's night-time and two eyes are looking at you. What kind of animal is it? Doodle it here.

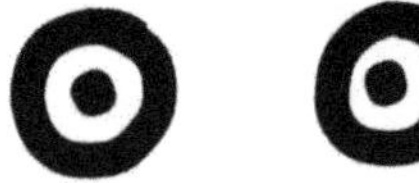

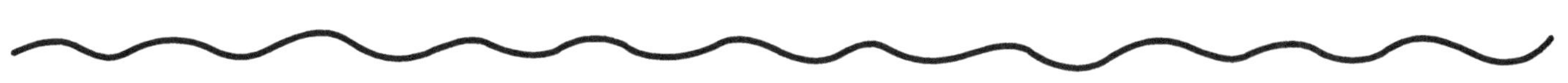

Dots and More Dots

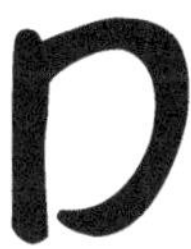ots can be used to fill blank spaces and outline pictures. Decorate these heart shapes and outline them with dots.

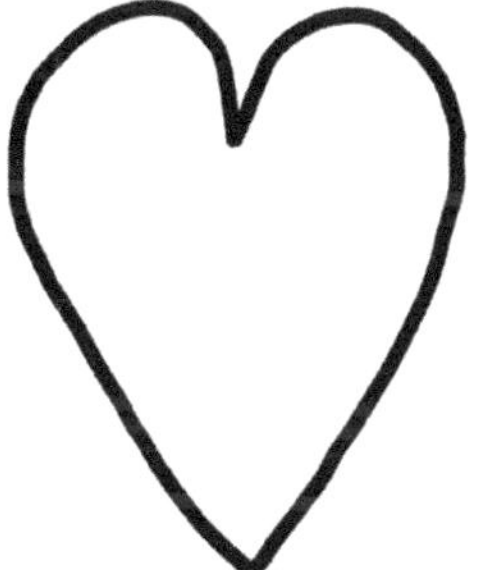 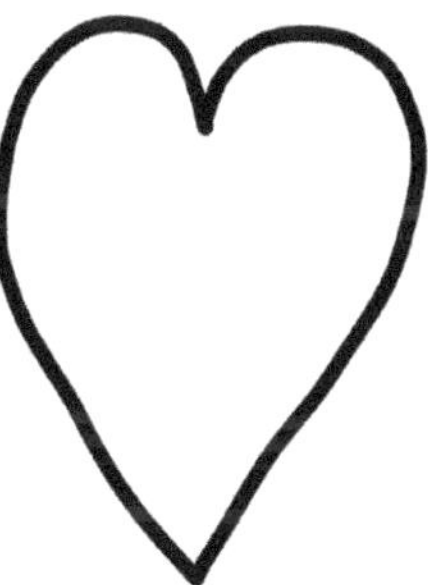 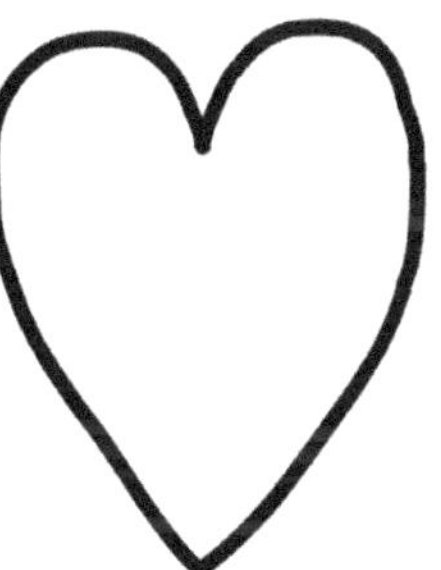 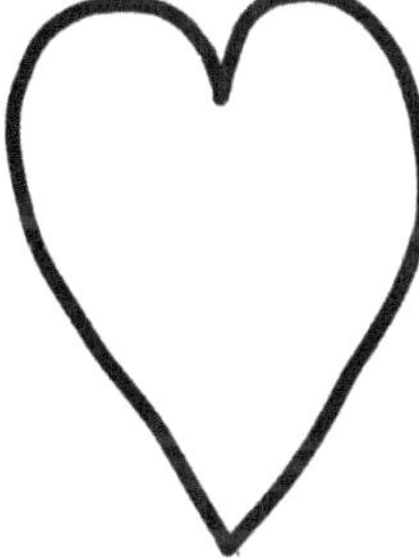

Double Outlining

Double outlining emphasizes the shapes and sizes of things. Add color to these shapes and outline them with lines, broken lines, or dots.

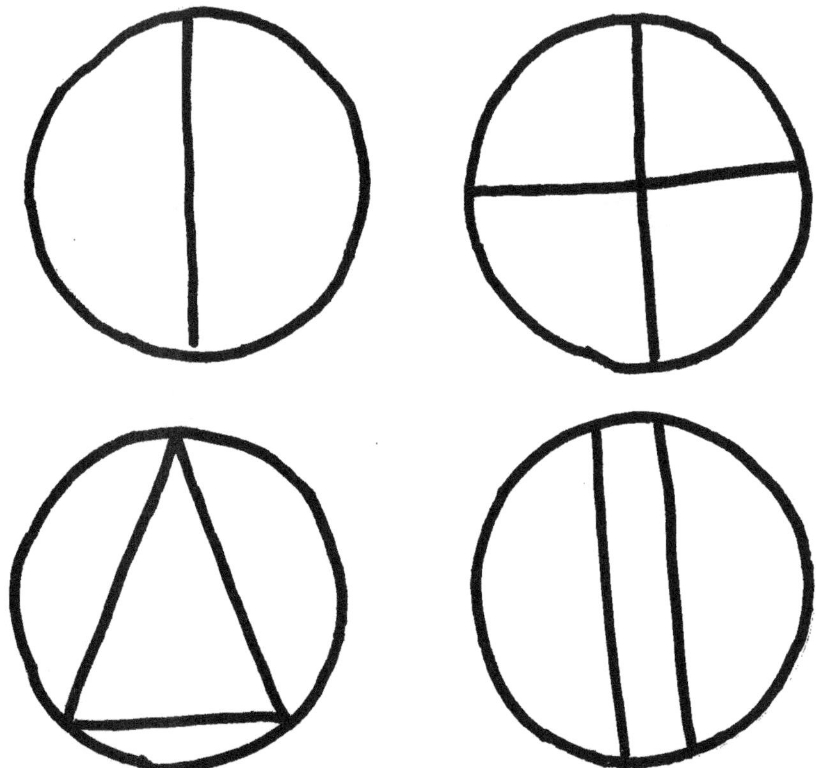

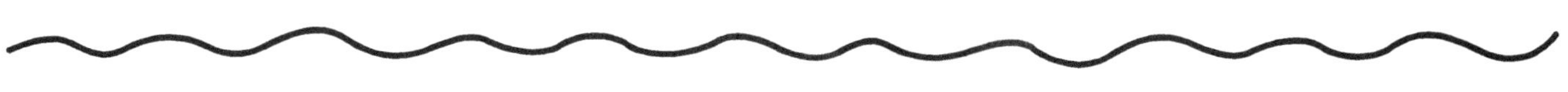

Zentangles

Z entangles are black drawings on square white paper. Using black, draw a curvy line inside the square. Fill both sides of the square with doodle shapes.

Landscapes

Crooked houses and anything near them are called Landscape Doodles. Doodle some crooked houses by this road. Add more details if you wish—flowers, trees, cat, etc.

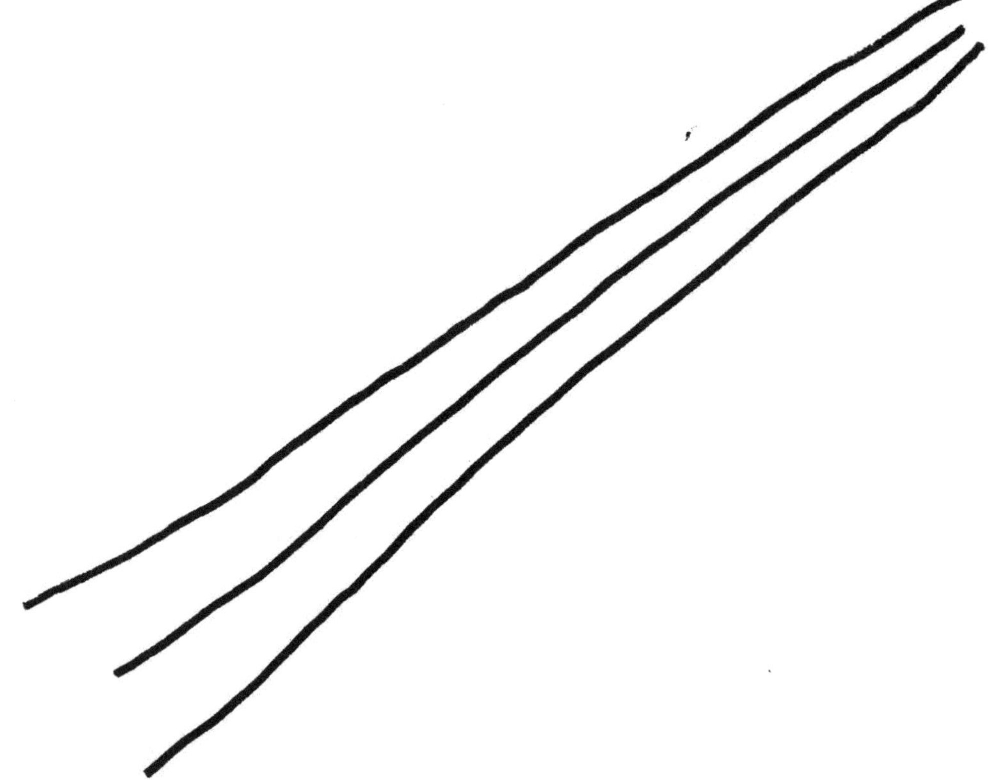

Freehand Mandala

The mandala, which means circle, originated in India. It begins with a center shape and uses repeat patterns. Draw concentric circles around the largest circle, leaving a little room between thm. Add shapes and patterns to each circle until your mandala fills the page.

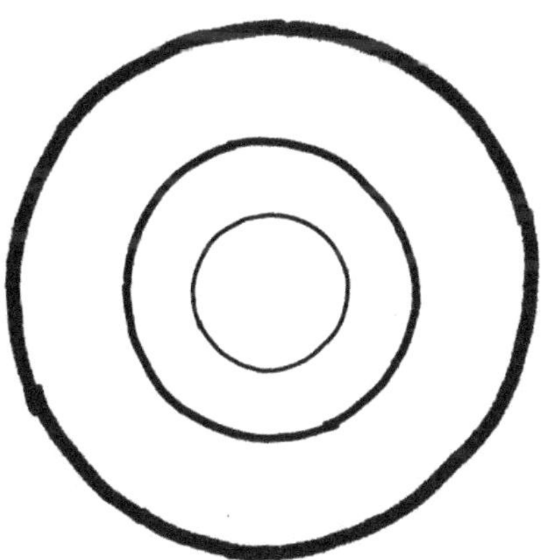

Popular Paisley

The paisley pattern, which has been around for centuries, is often used in doodle art. Fill this paisley shape with flowers, circles, dots, and lines.

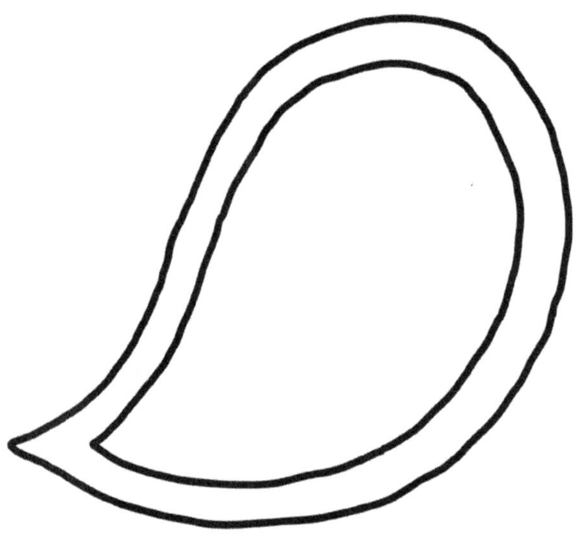

Dangles

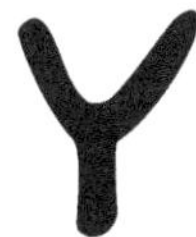ou may choose to add dangles to your doodle art. Study this example and make your own dangle with dots, lines, flowers, geometric shapes, and anything else you like.

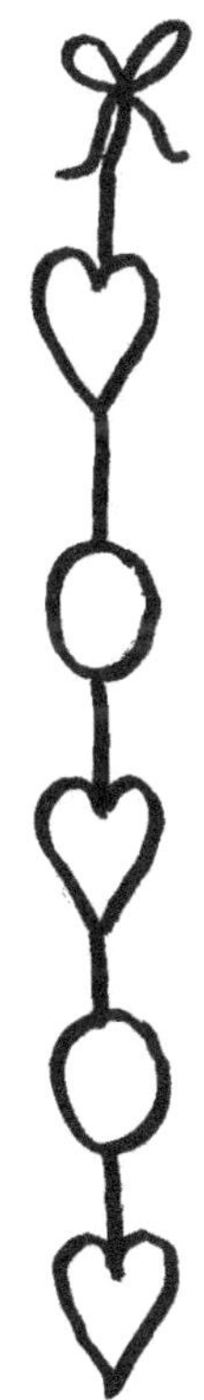

Finish the Bugs

Many doodle artists enjoy drawing insects. Finish these bugs with colorful doodle patterns. There's space for you to doodle more bugs, too.

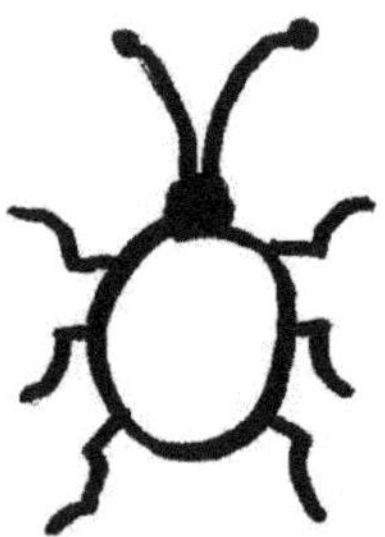 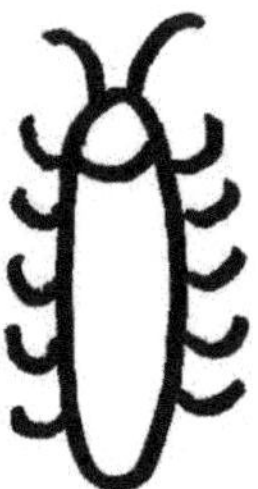 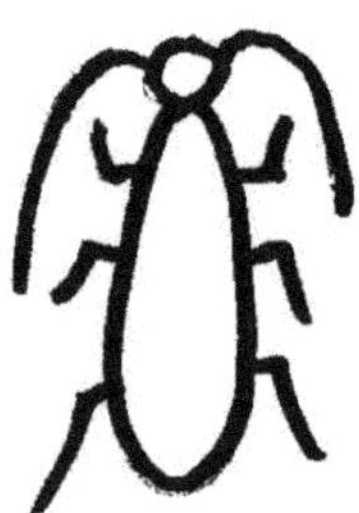

Small Changes, Big Results

Turn these circles into shining suns by changing the color of the circles, shape of the rays and adding different faces.

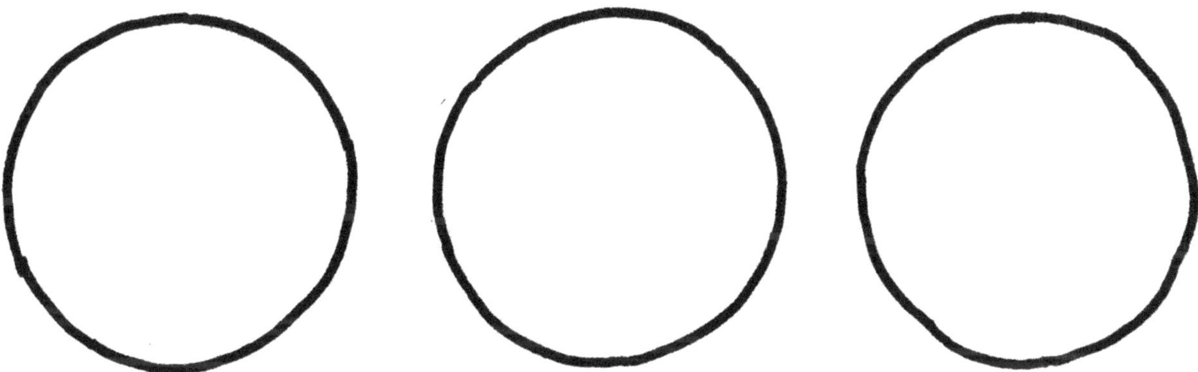

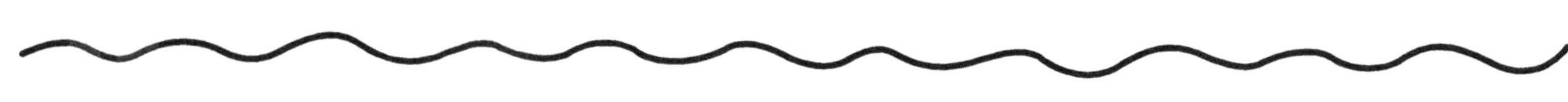

Spikes

Spikes can be a way to add movement and texture to doodles. Add different kinds of spikes—lines, dotted lines, triangles—to these shapes.

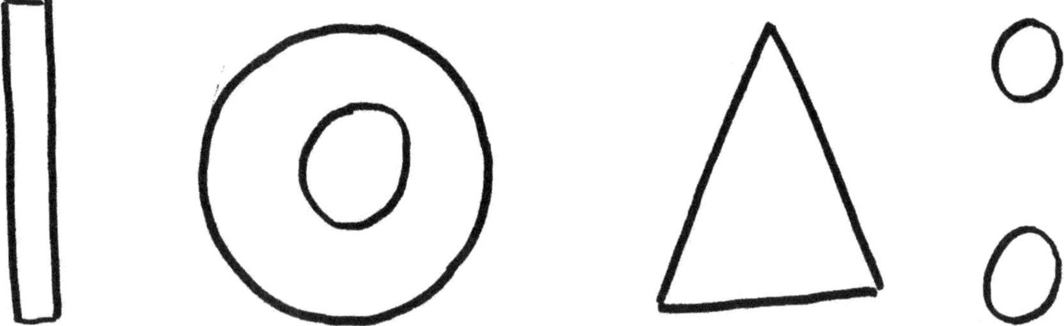

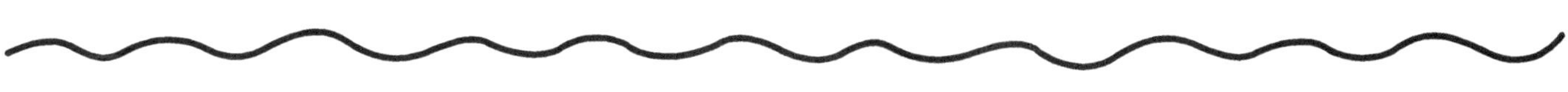

Grid

Connect the dots on this grid any way you want. Add colors to your grid doodle.

Doodle Letters

Make two fat letters here, the first letter of your first name, and the first letter of your last name. Decorate the inside of the letters with doodle patterns.

Simple Scribble

A dd more curves and swirls to this simple scribble. Finish it by adding color and pattern to each shape.

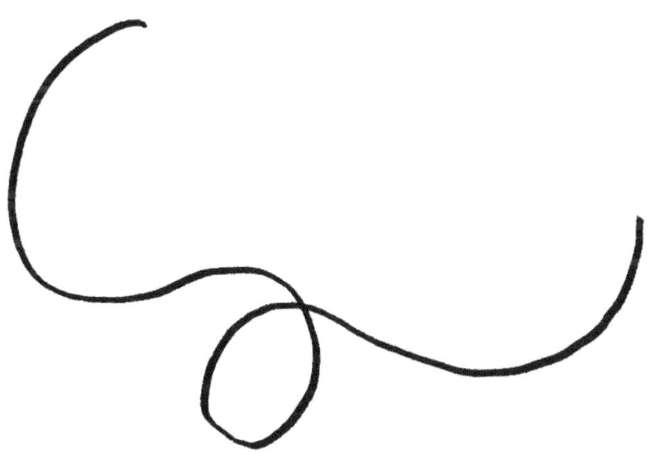

Complex Scribble

Add colors and repeat patterns to this complex scribble. You've created a work of art.

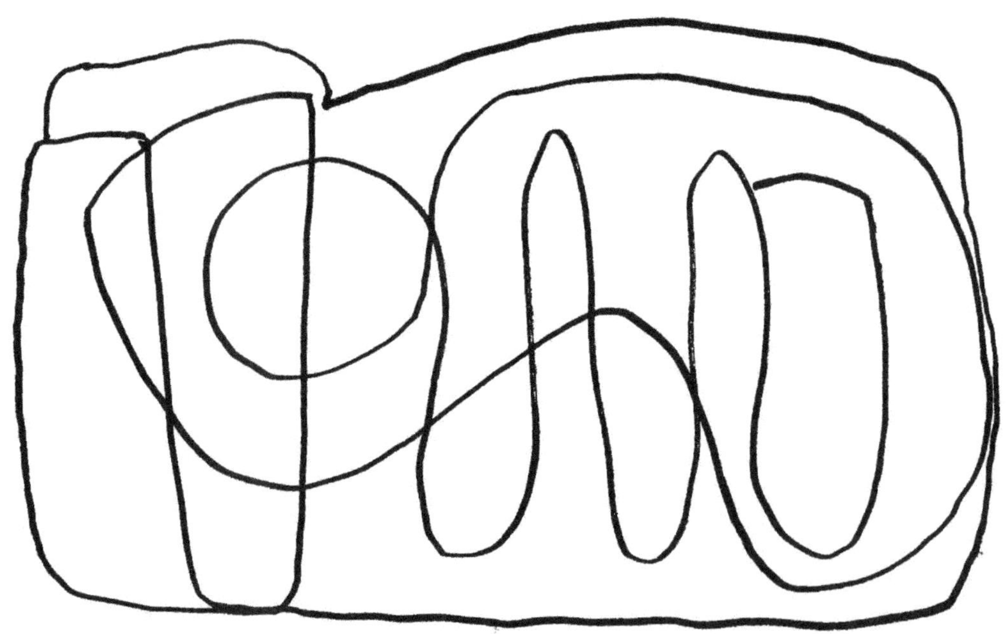

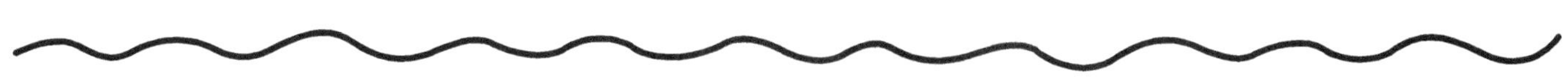

Silhouette

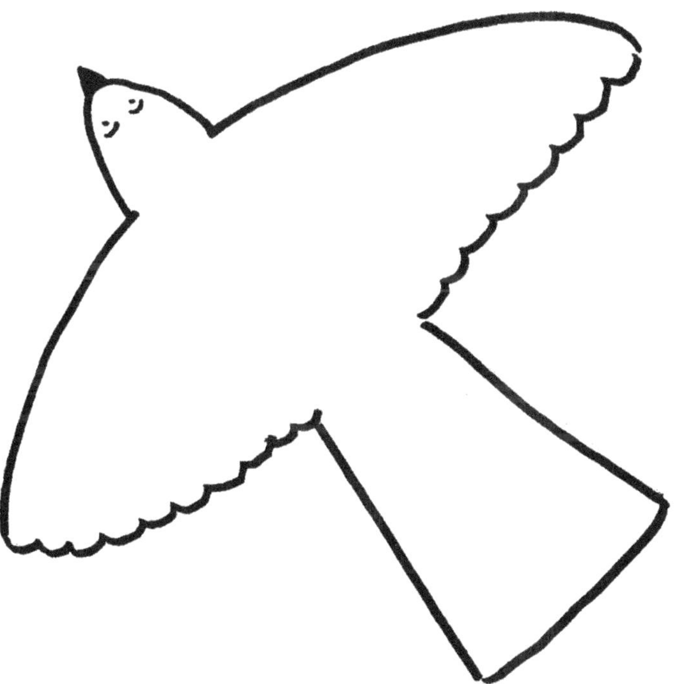

Silhouette doodles can be one color or many. Using different colors, add doodle patterns to the bird silhouette.

Borders

A border acts like a frame for doodle art. Borders can be straight, curved, or angular. Add color to these borders.

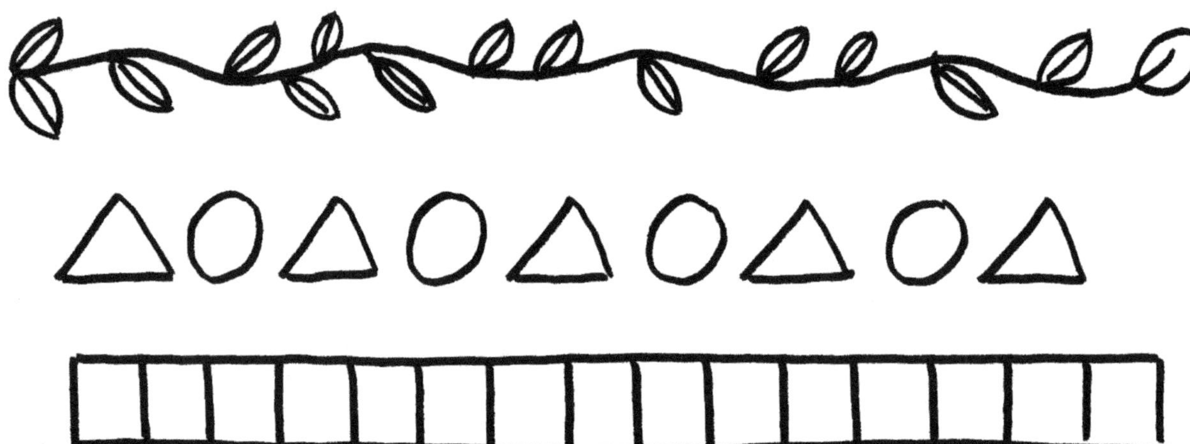

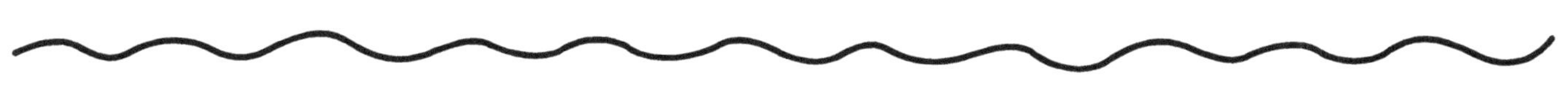

Border Frame

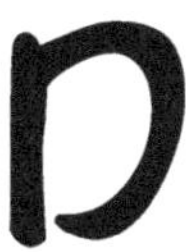oodle something or someone inside this empty frame. Then doodle a border around it.

Fillers

Alphabet letters, used in unusual ways, can be used to fill empty spaces and act as borders. Finish the U and V rows with the letters touching each other. Experiment with other alphabet letters. They can be right side up, upside down, or sideways.

U

V

Reverse Doodling

This idea may have come from an established doodling technique, watercolor wash. Paint blobs and shapes mixed with extra water are painted on watercolor paper. Doodle lines are added with black ink after the paint has dried. Turn these shapes into reverse doodles.

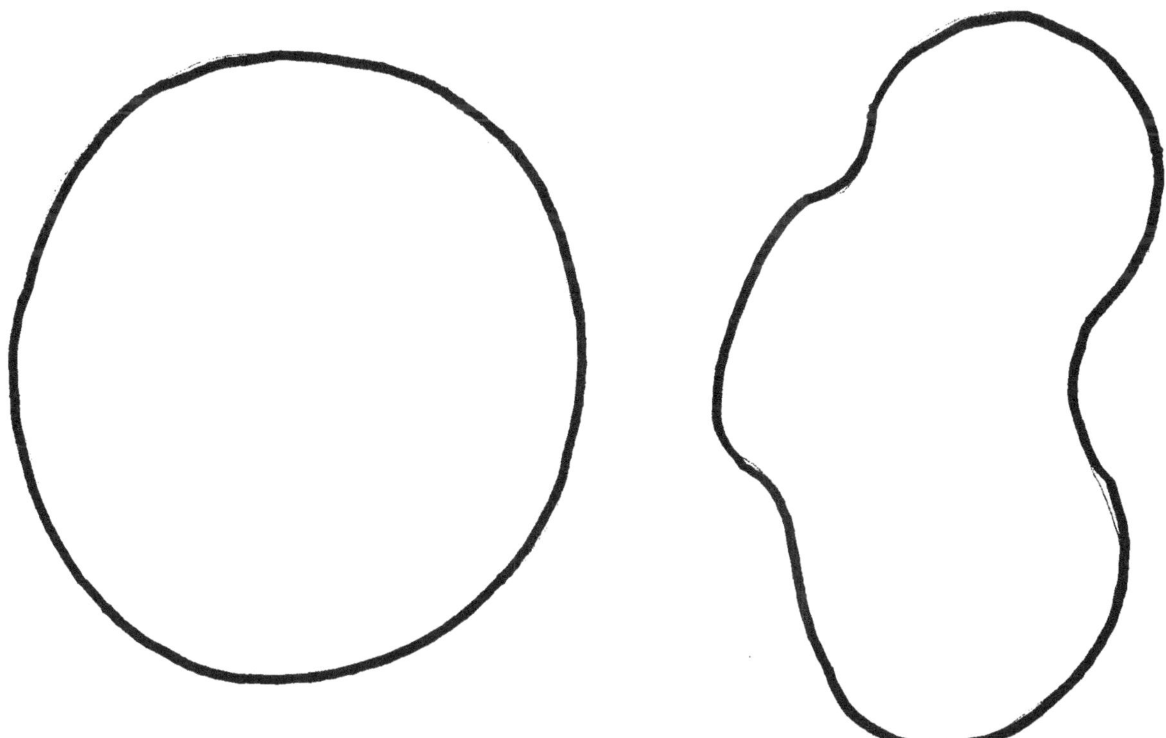

Your Link with History

Create a different doodle inside the squares of this tic-tac-toe. Like the cave person, you're a doodler, and this links you with those who lived thousands of years ago. How amazing!

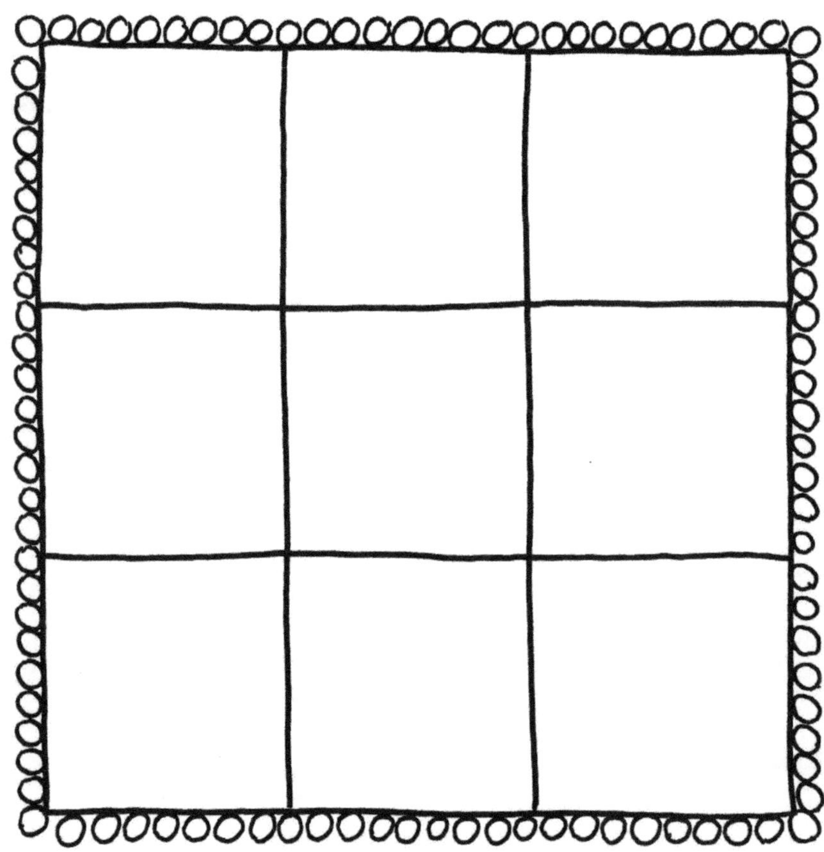

Part 9

Keep Doodling!

Now you know them—doodle art techniques and patterns—and are on your way. Keep doodling to feel more comfortable with this art form. The more you doodle, the better you will get.

I suggest buying a small pad and carrying it with you. Because normal pencil lines don't stand out, I use a black Flair felt-tip pen for doodles on the go. If I intend to mat or frame a picture, I do a pencil sketch first on watercolor paper, add color with permanent watercolors, and when the picture is totally dry, doodle lines with Black Pigment Micro Pens. The pens come in various tip sizes, which is a plus.

Adult coloring books are popular now and there are coloring clubs from coast to coast. You could start a doodling club. Invite family members or friends over and provide doodling materials. Though everyone uses the same techniques and patterns, the doodles will be quite different.

According to Sunni Brown, author of **The Doodle Revolution**, "Everyone has a signature doodle—the drawing that leaks out of us when we're not noticing." What's more, our doodles fall into specific categories.

- The Word Doodler remembers words and traces them repeatedly.

- The Nature/Landscape Doodler focuses on nature—trees, flowers, landscapes, and the outdoors.

- The Abstract Doodler likes geometric patterns and may create unrecognizable shapes.

- The People and Faces Doodler is preoccupied with figures and different expressions on human faces.

- The Picture Doodler creates recognizable images: people, objects, vehicles, animals, insects, etc.

Brown says these categories are part of your doodle DNA. I fit the Nature/Landscape category. What category do you fit? Your doodles may fit several categories, not just one. When you doodle, you're in the company of family, friends, strangers, and famous people.

These examples are from *Scrawl* by Caren, Claudia, and Todd Strauss-Schulson.

Artist Pablo Picasso doodled child-like suns. Author William Saroyan doodled colorful loops and scribbles. President Dwight Eisenhower doodled human figures, including himself. During World War II Winston Churchill doodled planes. Nurse Clara Barton doodled Red Crosses representing the organization she founded.

Humans have creative minds and use them differently. You probably know someone who "can fix anything" and is famous for this. That's their creative mind in action. A friend may be a fabulous baker and that's their creative mind in action. Another friend may be a "techie," at home with technology and its rapid changes.

Though you may not think of yourself as a creative person, there is natural creativity within you. You may spark this creativity by taking a walk, jotting down ideas that come to you, daydreaming, meditating quietly, and doodling. Make a promise to yourself: *I'll keep doodling and frame one of my favorite pictures.*

Doodling is creative, calming, surprising, and fun. Happy doodling to you!

The following ten pages are blank for you to create your own doodles using the samples in this book or creating your own patterns and techniques.

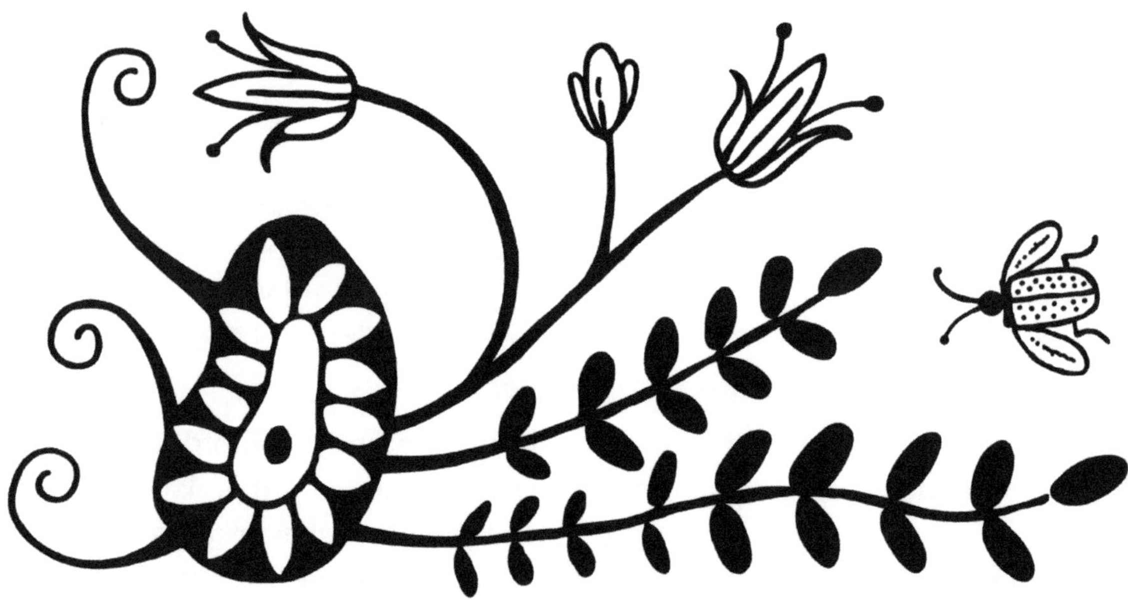

Resources

- Albert, Greg. "The Art of Scribbling," https://www.artistsnetwork.com>art-mediums-drawing

- Bleck, Diane, "Making Colorful Borders: Adding a Fun Frame to Your Doodles," https://doodleinstitute.mykajabi.com

- Brown, Sunni. *The Doodle Revolution*. New York: Portfolio, 2015.

- Fink, Joanne, "Creative Expressions of Grief" workshop, The Compassionate Friends National Conference, July 7-9, Denver, CO, 2023.

- Fink, Joanne. *Zenspirations: Letters and Patterning*. East Petersberg, PA: Fox Chapel Publishing, 2011.

- Geggel, Laura. "The World's Oldest Drawing is a 73,000-Year-Old Hashtag," https://www.livescience>63565-worlds-oldest-drawing-

- Hasenfratz, Carolyn. "Variations on Scribble Art," https://www.chasenfratz.com>variations-on-scribble-art

- Norton, Kendra. The Reverse Coloring Book. New York: Workman Publishing, 2021.

- Pillay, Srini, MD. "The Thinking Benefits of Doodling," Harvard Health Publishing, December 25, 2016, https://health.harvard.edu/blog/the-thinking-benefits-of-doodling-2016121510844

- Seuss, Emily. "Zentangle Art 101, https://emilyseuss.com>zentangle-art-a-beginners-guide

- Sokol, Dawn DeVries. *Doodle Zen: Finding Creativity and Calm in a Sketchbook.* New York: Abrams, 2016.

- Sosnoski, Karen, "Mental Health Benefits of Doodling and Drawing," https://www.healthline.com/health/mental-health-benefits-doodling

- Starr, Jeffrey. "Maria Thomas and Rick Roberts' Zentangles: A Worldwide Phenomenon." www.golocalworcester.com/lifestyle/maria-thomas-and-rick-roberts-zentangles-a-worldwide-phenomenon/#:~:ext=MariaThomas and Rick Roberts%2

- Steinberg, Saul, Saul Steinberg Foundation, https://saulsteinbergfoundation.org/search-artwork/page/3/

- Strauss-Schulson, Caren, Claudia and Todd. *Scrawl: An A to Z of Famous Doodles,* New York: Rosetti International Publishing, 2019.

- Tart, Sparkle (penname). "The 5 Styles of Doodling," https://sparkletart.com/rsr/2016/08/what-are-the-5-different-styles-of-doodling.html

- The Doodle Institute. "Making Colorful Borders: Adding a Fun Frame to Your Sketchbook," https:doodleinstitute.mykajabi.com/blog/making-colorful-borders

- Thanea (no last name). "How to Draw a Mandala," http://art-is-fun.com/how-to-draw-a-mandala

- Thorp, Clare, "From Da Vinci to Churchill: What our Doodles can Mean," https://www.bbc.com/culture/article/20210823-from-da-vinci-to-churchill-what-our-doodles-can-mean

- Tullet, Herve. *Draw Here: An Activity Book.* Handprint/Chronical Books LLC (2015), Bayard Editions (2018).

- Wilson, Clare. "World's First Drawing is a Red Crayon Doodle Made 73,000 Years Ago." https://www.newscientist.com >article >mg23931953

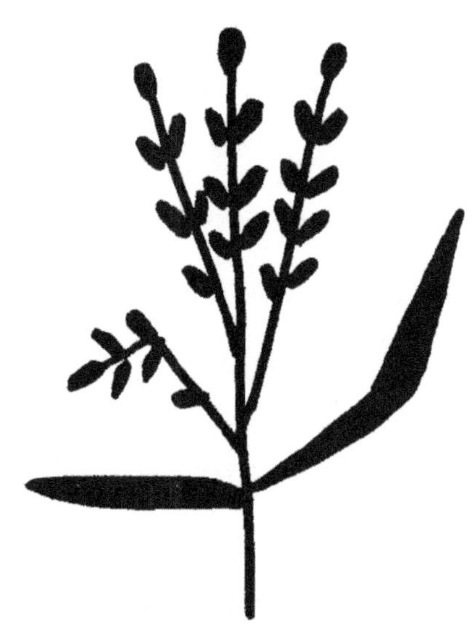

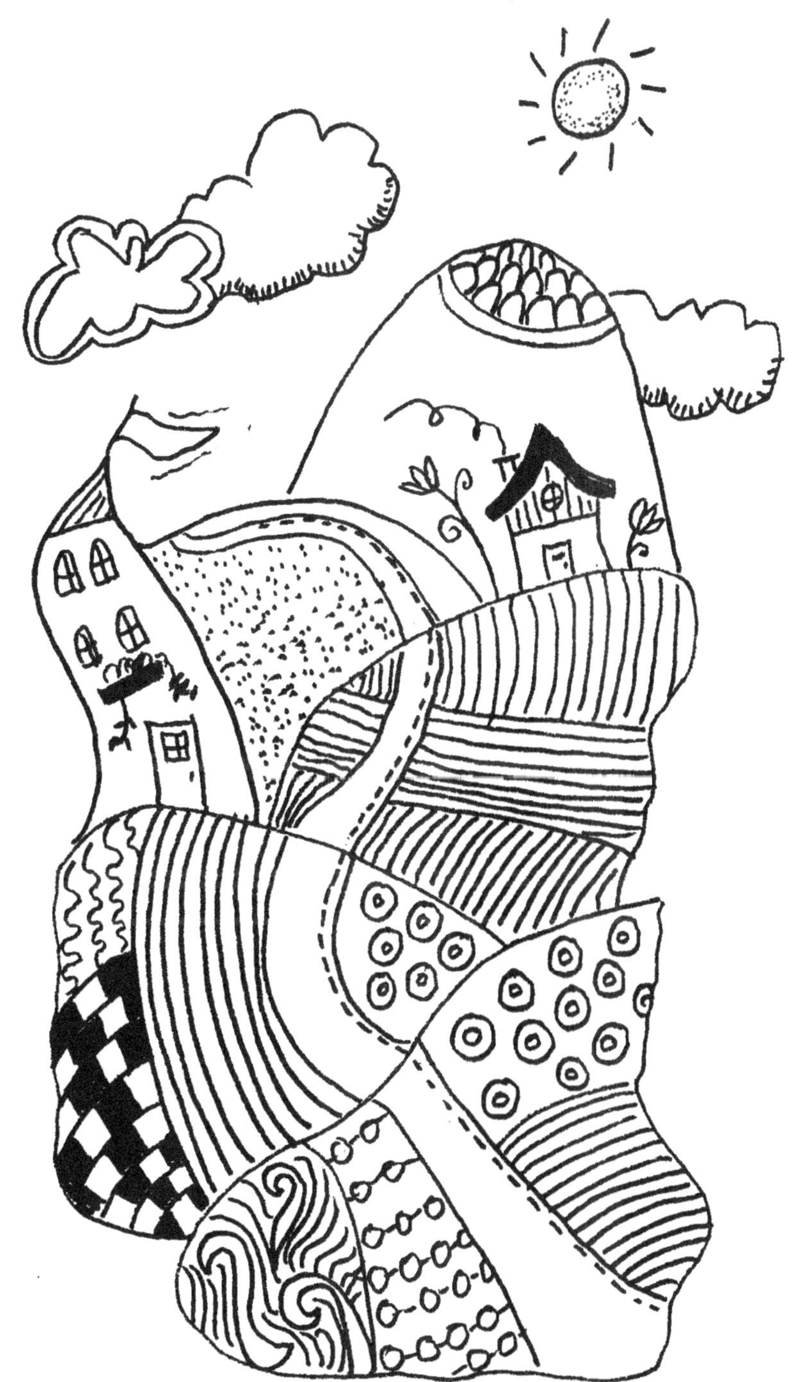

About the Author

Harriet Hodgson has been a freelance writer for decades, is the author of countless print and online articles and 48 books. She has a B.S. in Early Childhood Education from Wheelock College of Education and Human Development at Boston University and an M.A. in Art Education from the University of Minnesota. Hodgson is also a certified art therapy coach and doodle artist. This photo was taken in her studio.

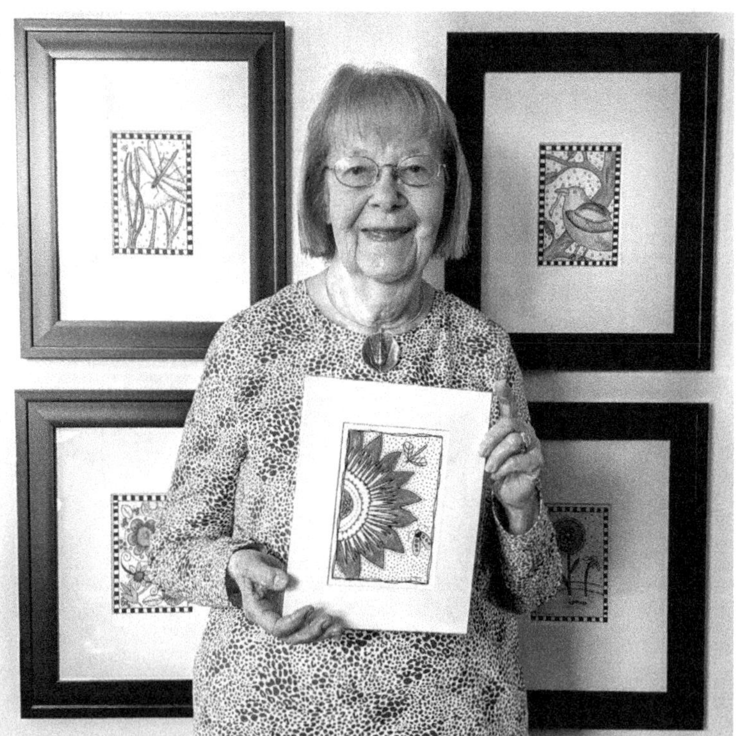